KINGDOM COURTING

Dana Tyler

This work is dedicated to my wonderful daughters
Danielle and Gabrielle Gill.
I love you with all of my heart.
The only One Who loves you more is Jesus.
Everything that I can't do for you, He will.

PREFACE

This book was derived from the notes of a series that I teach called "How to Court in the Kingdom". The attendees usually receive an outline and we discuss each of the segments in this book. Many have been blessed by the teaching and encouraged me to publish my teaching notes, so I decided to flesh out the skeletal outline and put my thoughts into print the way I teach them. This handbook is a combination of my thoughts and a compilation of materials I gathered from other sources. Since the publishing of this book, we have now designed a full conference called Kingdom Courting University. My greatest desire for you is that you come away comfortable with your season as a single person with a better understanding of yourself, your relationship with God and why you are seeking a spouse. I pray what you read will be encouraging, thought provoking and life changing. May the Lord bless you on your introspective journey and guide you into finding your special someone.

ABOUT THE INSTRUCTOR

Minister Dana Tyler serves as the singles director for the Holiness is Hott Singles' Coalition, a division of the Shield of Faith Fellowship of Churches, International. Dana is currently pursuing her Doctorate of Theology from Liberty University, in Virginia with a minor in Christian Counseling. She has two beautiful, anointed and gifted daughters, Danielle and Gabrielle. She currently resides in Southern California where she soaks up the sun at Newport Beach every chance she gets. Her teaching style is witty, humorous, energetic and very candid. She loves Jesus with all of her heart, soul and strength and she loves His people.

For more information on Dana, her upcoming engagements and other projects visit: **www.danatyler.me**

Follow Dana on Instagram, Twitter and Periscope @danadtyler
Connect with Dana on www.facebook.com/Dana.Tyler.33

TABLE OF CONTENTS

INTRODUCTION   11

COURTSHIP DEFINED   15

WHAT IS THE DIFFERENCE BETWEEN DATING   AND COURTING?   19

BIBLICAL COUPLES TO CONSIDER WHEN COURTING   23

15 TIPS TO CONSIDER FOR SUCCESSFUL COURTING   33

CONFUSING SEX WITH LOVE   41

BREAKING UP IS HARD TO DO   45

BASIC SOCIAL ETIQUETTE   49

SINGLE NOT ALONE   53

WHAT DOES IT MEAN TO BE EQUALLY YOKED?   57

CONCLUSION   63

LOVE LANGUAGE QUIZ   69

8 BASIC ETIQUETTE RULES THAT EVERYONE SHOULD FOLLOW   73

SEXUAL ATHEISM   77

POWER OF DELAYING GRATIFICATION   83

DELAY OF GRATIFICATION AND EXCEPTIONAL MARRIAGES   87

PERSONALITY TEMPERAMENT TEST   91

INTRODUCTION

Many Christian singles seem to be bound in loneliness and depression by misconceptions of what they believe about themselves and about marriage from-believe it or not- what they've learned in church! I never realized the stigma attached to being single, particularly in the House of God, until after my husband passed away. Too many times, I have been asked "Why are you single?" as though being single was the worst thing on the planet. I found myself trying to find reasons and justify why I was not married and came up empty, mostly, because I never looked at my life as being deficient simply because I was no longer married. It opened my eyes to the plight of the single men and women around me, some of whom had never been married and desperately wanted to marry. In examining the motivation for marriage among my contemporaries, I started to find that the people of God needed better direction concerning how to view friendships, relationships, love and marriage in a Christian environment.

After becoming the singles director for my church, my greatest desire is to see singles made whole and healthy before they join in matrimony with another. It is my mission to help singles recognize that their future marriage isn't just a fairy tale come true. It is actual ministry and does not just impact them, but the world. God uses marriage to build His Kingdom! The hope is that, armed with sound biblical principles, those desiring marriage will take a little more care in choosing a spouse, developing themselves and preparing to *be* the right spouse and recognize the significance of the relationship in which they choose to participate.

It is also my deepest desire to help repair and build the esteem of those who have fallen prey to the lie that "you are nobody until somebody loves you"; to debunk the myth that marriage is the key to happiness, and to assure you that neither sexual immorality nor loneliness has to be your experience simply because you are single. Trust me. I know how great the pressure is to be married. I feel it constantly from my parents, my pastor and my peers. I also know that pressure to please God supersedes their desire or even my desire to be married.

It is no news for you, Christian single, that whether you like it or not, your pastor wants to you to be married. He or she does not want to see you to live in sexual sin or be emotionally frustrated. Yet, how many times have you heard other singles declare, "It is better to marry than to burn?" as justification for why they are in a hurry to get married.

We have been conditioned to get married because we believe we cannot or choose not to control our sexual desires. Too many Christians end up marrying simply because they want to have sex legally and they are totally unprepared for how to sustain that marriage successfully. We want to live in obedience to God and that is wonderful. But what happened to producing the fruit of the Spirit, one part of which is temperance, or self-control? Often, we do not stop to really consider all of the components of marriage that have nothing to do with sex. The act of getting married just to keep from sinning is church thinking.

Can I also share with you that your pastor recognizes that good, godly marriages build strong families. Strong families build strong churches. Strong churches build strong communities. Strong communities impact a nation. A strong nation impacts the world. If there is anything this nation needs more of, it is godly marriages between one man and one woman. America is in dire need of families who raise children in the "fear and admonition of the Lord" and look at the world through the lenses of Truth which is the Word of God. Marrying knowing that your marriage will produce the will of God is kingdom thinking.

You are reading this book because you want to elevate your relationships from church thinking to kingdom thinking. You do not simply want to marry someone for the sexual benefits that marriage provides but for all of the rights and responsibilities that the covenant of marriage entails. You want to develop sound, healthy relationships and adequately prepare for a marriage that will last.

This book is designed to get you to really evaluate yourself, your motives for marriage, the quality of people you are attracting to your life, whether they are helping you produce what God wants to produce in your life; help you develop or improve the fruitful relationships and end the ones that are ultimately detrimental to your destiny. When you begin to recognize that God has a greater purpose for your marriage, you will stop allowing yourself to be connected to the wrong people out of desperation. I want to help you learn to please God in every stage of your relationship from, "Hello, my name is…" to "I do."

Let's get started on our journey for courting the Kingdom way.

COURTSHIP DEFINED

What is courtship? It seems like such an archaic term to use. One immediately thinks of arranged marriages and women in corsets sitting on fainting couches. Wikipedia simply defines courtship as the "period in a couple's relationship which precedes their engagement and marriage, or establishment of an agreed relationship of a more enduring kind. During courtship, a couple gets to know each other and decides if there will be an engagement or other such agreement. A courtship may be an informal and private matter between two people or it may be a public affair, or a formal arrangement with family approval. Traditionally, in the case of a formal engagement, it has been perceived that it is the role of a man to actively court or woo a woman, thus encouraging her to understand him and gauge her receptiveness to a proposal of marriage." (Wikipedia)

[COURTSHIP DEFINITION: A PERIOD DURING WHICH A COUPLE DEVELOP A ROMANTIC RELATIONSHIP, ESP. WITH A VIEW TO MARRIAGE.

ROMANCE DEFINITION: A FEELING OF EXCITEMENT AND MYSTERY ASSOCIATED WITH LOVE.

AFFECTIONATE DEFINITION: READILY FEELING OR SHOWING FONDNESS OR TENDERNESS.]

I like the above Webster's Dictionary definitions of courtship, romance and affectionate because all of them refer to developing relationship intimacy but not to sex. It is something I want you to keep in mind when cultivating relationships. What I really want you to think about when it comes to courting and its definition is that marriage is the ultimate goal in a specified relationship and that the relationship should be conducted in a wholesome manner. Now, every relationship you cultivate is not going to end in marriage; however, all of them, especially the one that does end in marriage should be sound, godly, friendships.

While some of your relationships will be romantic, remember romance is the feeling of excitement and mystery associated with love. If you are a marriage-minded Christian single, I would like you to consider all of the ways to explore the mysteries of loving someone without being driven by sexual feelings. You are sure to develop great, lasting friendships when you stop looking at every member of the opposite sex as a potential bedmate. Learn to develop intimate friendships where you are affectionate first then courting and marriage can be the by-product. Please note that nowhere in the definition of being affectionate is there sexual implications. Unfortunately, we live in a society of people who confuse romance with sex and sex with love. But we'll discuss that in a later chapter. For now, let's look at the difference between dating and courting.

WHAT IS THE DIFFERENCE BETWEEN DATING AND COURTING?

In my view, dating is a little more casual, exploratory and non-committal than courting. Dating is typically that stage right between friendship and courtship. There is one or more person with whom you desire a more intimate relationship than simple friendship. You go on a series of dates, hang out, your friendship deepens, but you are not necessarily on the path to marriage. At the dating stage, some would even suggest that you date a variety of people just to figure out the type of person you like and with whom you are compatible. I would strongly caution against dating multiple people from the same congregation, especially your own congregation. That stirs up entirely too much confusion and potential hostility if the relationship ends.

Courtship implies the exclusivity that dating just does not. When you are courting, you have narrowed it down to one potential candidate for marriage. That does not mean that you are engaged or that you behave as though you are married; it just means that you have selected someone with whom you believe marriage would be suitable. You both have the clear, mutual understanding that marriage is on the horizon and you are both making preparations toward that end. You have severed other relationships, incorporated prayer, counseling, and the guidance of a mentor or spiritual advisor. If you have children, they are now included in the formula. I often suggest that people with young children do not introduce their children into the relationship too soon so as to avoid confusion and emotional instability for the children.

Courtship puts the "burden of proof" on the man in that the man actively pursues the woman. Men, whether they are Christians or not, are hunters. However, we live in a society where women throw themselves at men so flagrantly, and have become the aggressors in relationships, that men either do not know how or do not have the opportunity to hunt for us anymore. Does that mean that the relationship is not reciprocal? Of course not! It does, however, allow for the restoration of right alignment in relationship for your future marriage if you get it right in the courting stage.

People date with all sorts of motives in mind, people court with the specificity of marriage in mind. As a Christian who is searching for a potential mate and seeking to please God while doing it, I encourage you to go from someone who has a dating mentality to someone who has a courting mentality. Singles courting with marriage in mind want to see the fulfillment of not just their personal desires, but God's will and desires for them. The difference between dating and courting is the difference between church thinking and kingdom thinking.

If you are dating just because you do not want to be alone, to have the satisfaction of knowing that someone loves you or because you feel pressure from family or the church to be married, you are in a relationship for the wrong reasons. We have a strong desire for companionship; God put that in us. It is only when that strong desire turns into desperation that we get into trouble and rush into relationships that are not right for us. I encourage you to examine your motives for marriage. Recognize that your potential marriage has greater significance than just your personal happiness. God certainly wants you to be happy, but He also wants to use your marriage to build His Kingdom.

In the next few pages, we will take note of some biblical couples and the greater purpose God had for their marriages. I wonder what purpose God has for your future marriage.

BIBLICAL COUPLES TO CONSIDER WHEN COURTING

JACOB AND RACHEL

Genesis 29: 17-21 "...but Rachel was beautiful and well favoured. And Jacob loved Rachel; and said I will serve thee seven years for Rachel thy younger daughter. And Laban said, it is better that I give her to thee, than that I should give her to another man: abide with me. And Jacob served seven years for Rachel; and they seemed unto him but a few days, for the love he had to her. And Jacob said unto Laban; Give me my wife, for my days are fulfilled, that I may go in unto her."

Though it was the marriage of Jacob and Leah that actually brought us the lineage that produced Messiah, the marriage of Jacob and Rachel got the whole ball rolling. Jacob thought he was just going to marry the beautiful girl he saw by a well. He had no idea of the legacy that God would produce from their union: twelve sons, twelve tribes and a Savior. If God did that with Jacob and Rachel's marriage, what could God possibly be looking to produce out of your marriage?

There are a few key things we should note of about the story of

Jacob and Rachel concerning courting. First of all, Jacob prepared financially for his future wife. He served for her and the Bible tells us that the years he labored for her seemed like a few days because of how much he loved her. He actually ended up working double time for her but he did it because he loved her. The primary response of loving is giving. "For God so loved the world that He gave..." (John 3:16)

As a side note, let me say this. God designed men to be givers as evidenced by their anatomy. Women are receivers and nurturers. We can only nurture whatever we have been given. Somewhere along the line, the tables have been turned and more men seem to be looking for what a woman can give them as opposed to what they have to give as a husband. I am not certain if it is the fear of being exploited by women who are solely looking for financial security or if it is the result of the shift in our culture.

As a kingdom son, you were designed to give. Do not be fearful of giving first and giving the most which does not only apply to finances. Give your time, your resources, your effort, your love and your open affection. Whatever you give to your future wife will be nurtured and returned to you, multiplied. It is the kingdom principle of sowing and reaping. If you sow negativity, skepticism and jealousy, guess what gets multiplied back to you. I promise you, better yet God promises you, that you cannot sow kindness, love, attention or even money without it being returned to you. You cannot be misused by walking in your divine purpose. Even if a relationship does not end in marriage, if you have treated God's daughter properly, He will be glorified in your life. Trust God to protect you and reward you accordingly. That is taking your thinking from church to kingdom.

Secondly, even though Rachel was beautiful and nicely built--that is what "well-favored" means-- there was no sexual contact between them for those seven years, save a chaste kiss. You can be physically attracted to someone and not engage in sexual activity. Jacob restrained himself for seven years without the Holy Ghost! The Lord always promises to "make a way of escape" when temptation comes. Listen to the Holy Ghost and be wise enough to recognize the way of escape and take it.

Thirdly, Rachel worked, too. Genesis 29:9 says "Rachel came with her father's sheep; for she kept them." Rachel had her own financial responsibilities and contributed to her household; she was industrious. Oftentimes, ladies fall into the trap of believing their husband being a provider means he has to be the sole bread winner. Clearly, the Lord values industrious women who work. Laziness is never listed as a virtue in Proverbs 31.

Lastly, Rachel was the gift, not Jacob. Genesis 2:22 tells us, "And the rib, which the LORD God had taken from man, made he a woman, and brought her unto the man." Man is not God's gift to woman. Woman is God's gift to man!

Gentlemen, she is the gift, not you! If you are interested in someone who does not make you value her as a gift, she is probably not the person to whom you should commit yourself. If anything either in her behavior or your attitude toward her does not make you feel blessed to be in her presence the majority of the time, either you need to change how you value her or change the interest you have in her and release her.

Ladies, you are the gift, not him. You ought not settle for anyone who treats you like anything less than the best gift, even in the dating and courting stages. Chivalry is not dead and there are men out there who recognize the value of a godly woman and treat her well. Recognize your value as a daughter of God's Kingdom and act accordingly.

AQUILA AND PRISCILLA

Not many people pay attention to this obscure tent-making couple, but Aquila and Priscilla had a major impact on building the early church and thus the Kingdom of God. They are an example of an equally-

[GOD HAS GREATER PURPOSE FOR YOUR POTENTIAL MARRIAGE THAN YOU BELIEVE] yoked, spirit-filled couple with a godly marriage that resulted in powerful ministry to the world.

In his essay, *Aquila and Priscilla, A Godly Marriage for Ministry*, Gordon Franz records that there are nine aspects of intimacy that most couples experience together: emotional, intellectual, aesthetic, creative, recreational, work, crisis, spiritual and sexual intimacy. These are some areas that you should take into consideration for your relationship. Note that sexual intimacy is just one of nine areas of intimacy a couple can experience. How many of these areas of intimacy are you cultivating in your friendships and potential romantic relationships?

Upon examining Aquila and Priscilla, we find they were perhaps the most perfectly matched couple in scripture that we hear the least about. Franz writes, "From what little information is recorded in the scripture, we can infer that Aquila and Priscilla experienced at least four of the nine aspects of intimacy. The first, spiritual intimacy is seen in the fact that their lives were centered around the Lord and His Church." They opened their home up to the local church and they entertained traveling preachers. They were with Paul for eighteen months. "Second, they shared work intimacy in making tents together. This was a family business in which they were both involved. Third, instructing Apollos shows their intellectual intimacy. They both knew the Scriptures and it is often implied that Priscilla took the larger role in ministry and in teaching because her name was mentioned first more often in the scriptures. Their names appear seven times in the New Testament. Finally, putting their life on the line for Paul's sake and moving for the sake of the gospel showed their crisis intimacy." Franz continues, "If Scripture had recorded more of the lives of these two saints, we would have seen more intimacy in their two-getherness."

I am certain Aquila and Priscilla had no idea that God would use their union to be such an integral part of building the early church. Imagine what kind of ministry God will build through your marriage. (Franz) **Acts 18, Romans 16:3-5 and I Corinthians 16:19-20**

ELKANAH AND HANNAH

Most of us know the story of Hannah and how she desperately wanted a child, but let's take a look at her husband, Elkanah. Elkanah had two wives: Penninah and Hannah. The Bible says he loved Hannah, even though she was barren. In that day, barrenness was an extremely shameful state and Hannah suffered great dishonor and ridicule from everyone except her husband because of his abiding love for her.

Scripture indicates that Elkanah was not only deeply concerned for his wife's happiness and treated her well, but that he loved and honored God. Hannah had made a vow to God that if He opened her womb and gave her a son, she would dedicate him to the service of the Lord. Elkanah, as Samuel's father, had the right to cancel the oath she had made, but he did not. He even allowed her to nurse the baby and bond with him before she put him into the Lord's service. God blessed the couple with three more sons and two daughters because they lent Samuel to Him. God pays with interest!

It can be implied that Elkanah was also a good father in that, Samuel, as an adult, made his home in Ramah which was the home of his father. This would indicate that Elkanah was a good father, maintaining a positive relationship with his son, despite Samuel living in Shiloh as a youth. Elkanah's only flaw seems to be his relationship with Peninnah who was particularly cruel to Hannah. However, it was Peninnah's taunting that drove Hannah to seek her refuge in the Lord. Through all of emotional turmoil in this marriage, God's greater purpose of bringing the nation of Israel the prophet Samuel was birthed from their union. Just imagine what God has planned for the children that are produced from your marriage! **I Samuel 1; 1 Samuel 2:1, 20-21**

ESTHER AND AHASUERUS

The marriage of Esther and Ahasuerus (Xerxes) is proof positive that God uses marriage to bring His purposes to pass. This is an example of a couple that was unequally yoked in every way, but God still had His hand in the marriage. A nation was spared because Esther recognized the greater significance of her marriage to King Ahasuerus. She could have been caught up by the trappings of the luxuries her marriage afforded her. If she did not rely on the Lord to know how to properly minister to her husband, she could not have interceded for her people. She fasted and sought the Lord for specific instruction on how to minister to her husband and gain his favor and thus fulfilled God's purpose for her marriage and not her own. I use this story to exemplify how to use spiritual means to minister to your spouse. When difficulties in marriage arise, you will have to be prepared to fast and pray for your spouse, your marriage and your family. **Book of Esther**

RUTH AND BOAZ

The Story of Ruth and Boaz is a common love story taught to single ladies as an inspiration to wait for our kinsman redeemer. This real life Cinderella story straight from the annals of biblical history inspires ladies to let their Boaz find them gleaning in the fields. I find it interesting that Boaz found Ruth in the fields, but Ruth found Boaz on the threshing floor. We have been taught that if we just keep working in the kingdom and mind our business, our Boaz will find us. But it was not until Ruth lay down at his feet on the threshing floor that Boaz decided to offer her the covering and the covenant of marriage. We know the significance of Boaz being the type of Jesus as our consummate Kinsman Redeemer. What can we learn from their story concerning marriage?

I was curious about the significance of the threshing floor, so I did a little research. The threshing floor is symbolic of many things. It is the picture of judgment. It is a place of blessing. It is a place symbolic of worship. It is also symbolic of the relationship between The Bride (Church) and the Bridegroom (Jesus).

A physical threshing floor is a large flat area where the wheat is separated from the husk which is where we get the picture of judgment. There are also two large, flat stones at the center of a threshing floor used to grind the grain. One stone rests on top of the other and they are fitted and joined together. The top stone is referred to as the female stone and the bottom stone is considered the male stone. The act of grinding the grain is a depiction of the act of marriage. It is no coincidence that Ruth found Boaz on the threshing floor, in the place of worship; in a place of humility (laying at his feet); in the place that is symbolic of the very institution that God uses to describe His relationship with His Church. Especially considering it was Ruth's love and commitment to God that led her to Boaz in the first place.

It is often taught that it is Ruth's work ethic that secured her marriage to Boaz, but I submit to you it was her worship ethic! I also submit to you that a husband was the by-product of having a right relationship with God and putting Him first. This is a classic example of a woman who sought the kingdom of God first and His righteousness and had all these things-a husband, a home, financial security, protection added to her.

I also love this story because there is a bit more to it than meets the eye. We often talk about being equally-yoked and this is a story of the unbelieving wife being sanctified by the believing husband or rather the believing husband's mother. Ruth did marry a man of faith and was converted but he was not the husband of "promise", if you will. Her first husband, if you recall, was Naomi's son, Mahlon, whose name means "invalid". Now, the definition of "invalid" happens to be two-fold in this case. It means both "sick" and "illegal, unenforceable, null & void". Mahlon was of the house of Judah and seemed to have all of the right qualifications; however, he died, and it was Boaz who became the patriarch whose line birthed David and eventually Jesus. Again, we see God's greater purposes at work in the earth through marriage. We can sometimes be convinced that someone meets all of the right qualifications, but God can have something totally different in mind. The key is to have a sincere relationship with God and be able to hear Him when He gives us instruction. **Book of Ruth**

Each of these couples faced and survived some of the same relationship issues you do: the pressure of ministry, jealousy, personal insecurity, death and tragedy, great emotional turmoil, yet God used each marriage for His purpose.

Now that we have examined the greater significance of marriage and how God has historically used the institution of marriage in scripture, let's talk about some practical ways we can ensure that we choose the appropriate spouse and court in a way that is pleasing to God.

15 TIPS TO CONSIDER FOR SUCCESSFUL COURTING

1) **Change your view of marriage.** *Most people plan for a wedding that only lasts a few minutes, rather than a relationship that is designed to last a lifetime. I can guarantee you, you are not thinking of marriage in its proper perspective. It is not your fault. Society has totally obliterated and degraded the covenant of marriage and even most pastors do not teach about it properly. Marriage is not just the legal means to have sex. Marriage is a sacred, divine, holy institution that models Jesus' relationship to the church. Marriage is a ministry. The purpose of marriage is to bring UNITY to the church, our community and the world and in building the Kingdom of God. God uses the institution of family to advance the Kingdom of God and restore to the earth what was taken from it when Adam and Eve sinned. It should not be entered into lightly. Your spouse will never fill the void in you that Jesus can. Pastor Paula White has a great video on You Tube entitled*

"Let's talk about it– Preparing for Marriage". Check it out.

2) **Know yourself: strengths, weaknesses and limitations.** *Know your "Cuckoo for Cocoa Puffs" button. If you cannot handle physical touch like kissing or holding hands then do not make that part of your courting life. Know your love language, temperament, your personality type and what personality type is compatible with yours. I have included a personality test and a love language test that can also help you understand your temperament and the way you give and receive love. Ask yourself if you are willing to be a step-parent. Do you have the capacity to be a caregiver to older parents or in-laws?*

3) **Establish boundaries.** *Boundaries are good! They keep good things in and bad things out. Think about what you will or will not accept in a relationship. Know what you will and will not do for love. I recommend reading Boundaries in Dating by Dr. Henry Cloud.*

4) **Maintain your standards.** *Do not compromise your standards just because the person you are with does not meet them. You will set yourself up for failure, frustration and disappointment if you do not stick to the standards that are non-negotiable. Be as equally-yoked as possible, recognizing that no one will be your perfect match, but as you grow together, you will be perfected together.*

5) **Come to a mutual understanding of your expectations.** *If you know you are not really ready for marriage, do not inflict yourself on anyone. Be clear when expressing your desires either from the relationship or the person with whom you are courting. It is not wise, nor is it kind, to get involved with someone who wants more from you and your relationship than you do. They can fall into the misconception that you are going to change your mind.*

6) **Build and explore <u>multiple</u> healthy, sound, godly friendships.** *You can find the fulfillment you need for companionship in good, sound friendships both male and female. The key is to surround yourself with positive people who encourage you in your walk with the Lord, who bring out the best in you and help you work out the worst in you. Give yourself ample candidates to choose from. Having good friends to help you heal in other areas will take the burden of fulfillment coming from one person.*

7) **Discuss the stage of your relationship at EVERY stage of your relationship.** *I teach a series about the 4 Ships:* **Fellowship** *which is general church socializing,* **Friendship** *which is closer one on one socializing both male and female,* **Courtship** *which is intimate socializing between a man and a woman and* **Covenant Relationship** *or marriage. When you make that transition from fellowship to friendship, from friendship to courtship, TALK ABOUT*

IT! "I like hanging out with you, can we be friends?" "We've been friends for a while, I am attracted to you. I'd like to know if you'd be interested in dating." "I would like to date you exclusively." "May I court you?" It sounds silly, but I can assure you that miscommunication and misunderstandings are far more painful than the embarrassment of stating clearly how you are feeling and risking rejection. If you have questions about what something means in your relationship, ASK! Communication is so imperative to a successful courtship and can avoid so much confusion and emotional pain. Of course, when the transition into marriage, or covenant relationship, comes there will be a ring!

8) **Pray God's Word over your future spouse/marriage.** *Pray what you want your marriage to look like biblically to be sure you are praying God's will and not just what your flesh wants. I created my own personal marriage confession of faith. It changes as I mature spiritually. I combed the scriptures for all of His "exceeding great and precious promises" and I pray them over me, my future husband, our children, finances, sex life and spiritual walk. You should customize one of your own. It will strengthen you and benefit you immensely just studying and searching the scriptures. You may even find that the Lord changes your desires as you do it. Do not be fooled, I still ask God if I can have a tall, nicely built, handsome husband! I certainly hope He says, "YES!"*

9) **Be what you want to attract.** *If you want someone who is honest, BE honest. If you want someone who is financially sound, BE financially sound. Keep in mind it is possible to attract what you fear easier than what you truly desire. If you want someone with a good work ethic, develop yours. This will not only cause you to attract a great spouse, it will prepare you to be a better spouse. The Bible tells us that "iron sharpens iron". As you improve, you will also help your potential mate improve, whether or not the relationship lasts.*

10) **Be creative.** *You have heard the phrase: "Necessity is the Mother of Invention". The lack of sexual intimacy ought to encourage you to find other ways to express your love and affection. Find ways to surprise your significant other. As stated earlier, romance is the excitement and the mysteries associated with love. There is so much to explore in a relationship other than sex. Creating ways to spend time with one another and truly learn one another is so valuable and rewarding. You cannot imagine the satisfaction that comes from connecting to another soul with the intention of loving them for the rest of your lives together. This intimate emotional, spiritual connection makes the physical joining that much more pleasurable and fulfilling when it does occur in God's timing.*

11) Look for the "sweetness" of courting. *Court with the innocence of a 1950's sixteen-year-old couple. Write little notes and give little gifts. Send a sweet text message to your significant other when you are thinking of him or her. Write a poem or copy one from a book if you are not gifted to write. Leave a nice message on his or her social media page. Ladies, remember men like romance, too.*

12) Be <u>prepared</u> to handle rejection with grace and maturity. *There is a chance that the person in whom you have taken an interest may not want to be in a romantic relationship with you. Perhaps, they enjoy your friendship but do not seek a more intimate relationship with you. It is very romantic to hear married couples who say, "The Lord told me that was my wife, or my husband." And while I am sure that happens, if you pursue someone in that vein, BE SURE YOU HAVE HEARD FROM THE LORD and NOT YOUR LOINS! You may also find that, after some time, the relationship is not what you anticipated. It is so important to handle rejection or disappointment with spiritual maturity. It will take prayer, the support of good friends and careful consideration to execute this step properly. Developing and maintaining interpersonal relationships is so crucial and fragile, particularly in the Body of Christ. You do not want to ruin future dealings with someone and you do not want to embarrass anyone or make them uncomfortable to be around you. Do not get mad and leave The*

Church if someone does not want to be in a relationship with you or if you break up with someone. You do NOT want to harbor any feelings of resentment or unforgiveness. It is hard to sing on the worship team together when you have a grudge.

13) **Be financially sound.** *If you have bad credit, FIX IT. If you have good credit, SAVE. If you already save, INVEST. We all have room to improve our finances. Gentlemen, she should not have to pay for her dates with you. This lets her know you are financially prepared to take care of her. Ladies, be prepared to split the bill or treat him to a date on occasion. This lets him know, you are not a gold-digger. Every date does not have to be extravagant but RED BOX should not be the only option.*

14) **Always consult your pastor or spiritual mentor about who you are courting.** *Your pastor may know some things about the person you are pursuing. It is always good to have someone with an objective eye AND spiritual insight to examine your relationship. When you are in it, you are too close and your judgment can be clouded. Be willing to accept his or her counsel.*

15) **Recognize the biggest part of courting is learning delayed gratification.** *I have included a couple of articles about Christian dating and abstinence and delayed gratification. Your entire life as a saved person is all about delayed gratification. We are*

temporarily causing our flesh to suffer by denying it the sinful behavior it wants, for the greater reward of ALL the PLEASURE of living with Jesus forever. Courting the kingdom way is the same principle.

Remember: Part of the fruit of the Spirit is temperance. Exercising temperance in your relationship will not only bring God glory, it will increase your overall spiritual walk. Here are a few scriptural references concerning temperance: Galatians 2:22-23, I Corinthians 9:27. Titus 2:12 2 Peter 1:5-6 and Romans 13:14

CONFUSING SEX WITH LOVE

As Christian believers we have been taught that sex is only to be enjoyed inside the marital covenant but no one really understands why this is so. Sure, we have been told it is a sin but somehow we manage to justify this particular sin above all others. After all, we have these urges and God put them in us, so clearly He knows and understands our human frailty when we give into our baser nature. What we fail to realize is that there is so much more that goes along with sexual intimacy than just our physical pleasure. Again, it goes to looking at purpose and what God intended sex to do.

I think the reason most people, married or single, continue in sexual sin is because for the longest time the church has taught that sex is for the express purpose of reproduction which could not be further from the truth. You can have sexual intercourse a million times and never produce a child. Just ask Abraham and Sara; so, there goes that theory. Even if you have produced children, you certainly do not refrain from sexual activity just because the mandate to be "fruitful and multiply" has been fulfilled. So, if sex is not just intended for reproduction, or solely for our physical pleasure, what *is* God's purpose for sex and why should it only be for those who are married? First, we have to examine what actually transpires during sexual intercourse.

God is a brilliant Designer. You are a triune being; you are body, soul and spirit. When you have sex there is a physical exchange, a soulical exchange and a spiritual exchange. In the physical exchange, your body produces a hormone called oxytocin. Oxytocin is a tremendously powerful bonding hormone. It is released when you kiss or hug a loved one, when a man or woman is sexually aroused and when a mother nurses her baby. In fact, this hormone is so powerful it acts as an instant pain reliever for a woman who has just given birth. The extreme potency of this bonding hormone allows this new mother who has endured thirty-three hours of labor and eight stitches with no anesthesia to forget the pain of childbirth and connect with the little creature that has literally just ripped her body in two. Pharmaceutical companies have reproduced oxytocin as a pain killing narcotic. It is this same hormone that is released when a mother nurses her newborn child and further solidifies their bonding each time she nurses. Now, translate the power of this hormone to a sexual relationship.

Oxytocin is known as the monogamy hormone because it produces feelings of psychological and emotional stability for one person. When oxytocin is released during sexual intercourse, it actually programs the brain to love the person with whom they are having sex. The more times the hormone is released, the more the feeling of love is reinforced. Isn't that a beautiful transaction designed by a loving God? It makes perfect sense for a husband and wife to reinforce feelings of love through sexual intercourse, it is the reason it is called lovemaking. The other aspect of the physical act of making love is an exchange of energy. The law of physics tells us that energy is neither created nor destroyed, merely transferred. The physical exchange of energy between a husband and wife through sex should happen so many times that the energy becomes blended and you cannot tell which energy belongs expressly to the husband or to the wife. In biblical terms it is how these "two become one flesh". Isn't God brilliant!

Why, then, do we have so much emotional turmoil, infidelity, mistrust and dysfunctionality in our relationships? The answer is simple. Whenever you use something for a purpose other than its original function, design or intent you have perverted it. Sex outside of marriage, whether it is fornication or adultery, is a perversion of God's intent for it. Why? It is because God intended sexual intercourse to bind a husband to his wife and a wife to her husband. When you have multiple sexual partners, your essence has been splintered. You have tethered yourself to people God never intended you to be connected to and lost a portion of who you are. Now, an act that was designed to bring unity, love and trust to a couple, because it has been perverted, brings division, pain and mistrust.

In the spirit, you have created a soul tie. A soul tie can be positive and it can be negative. The Bible tells us that Jonathan's soul was knit to David's in I Samuel 18:1 as an example of a positive soul tie. Jonathan developed godly love, affection and brotherhood with David even though Saul, Jonathan's father, despised him. Genesis 34:3 tells us about Shechem's sexual soul tie to Dinah in an ungodly relationship where he was so consumed by lust that he raped Dinah. Think of a soul tie as an invisible conduit that now allows spirits to transfer between two people. If you have multiple sexual partners, you have literally tethered yourself in the spirit, not just to them but the people with whom they have had sex. Just as you can acquire a sexually transmitted disease, you can acquire a spiritually transmitted disease. Seemingly inexplicably, you will develop a desire for pornography that never existed for you before. Or, your temper is a problem for you when you never struggled with anger issues before. The problem is that most soul ties do not manifest themselves for years and you can no longer discern what sin habits were your original issues and what proclivities you have inherited from the person with whom you have had sex.

Often, we believe that if we have not contracted a physical disease or our encounter did not result in an unwanted pregnancy that we have escaped the dangers of having illicit sex. That could not be further from the truth. The fact of the matter is that we have reaped a greater consequence to ourselves than we believe. In fact, the Bible tells us that he that commits fornication sins against his own body. We are forced to fight greater emotional and spiritual battles than had we simply learned to manifest the fruit of the spirit. The great news is that from this moment on, you can recommit yourself to sexual purity and master your flesh. It will take fasting, prayer and spiritual warfare to overcome, but it can be done.

BREAKING UP IS HARD TO DO

Another question that is prevalent among singles that I have been asked to address a great deal is how to know when you are in the wrong relationship and how to get out of it. First of all, recognize that breaking up is hard to do even in the best of circumstances. No matter how long you have been in a particular relationship, letting go of the one you love, whether you have loved them three days, three weeks, three years or three decades is difficult for two reasons. The first is quite simply that loss hurts. Loss of love, loss of friendship and intimacy, loss of hope for your future together just plain hurts. The second reason is that it makes you doubt your worthiness of love or causes you to fault find. "What did I do wrong?" "Why didn't she love me enough to make our relationship work?" "Where did we go wrong?"

There are a number of reasons that relationships do not last and it does not necessarily mean there is anything wrong with either one of you, just that you may not be right for one another. The timing of your relationship may not be right. You may be in different places emotionally or the relationship may simply progress too quickly. There is no fault to be found in any of that but it is very easy to assign blame.

Now, do not get me wrong. There are some people out there, who whether they are believers or not, are just plain malicious manipulators. They are predators in relationships and you should be extremely cautious of them. We are talking about the gold diggers, those who are looking solely for sexual relationships, those who want to dominate you in a relationship and those who are outright psychologically, emotionally, verbally or physically abusive. Being in the wrong relationship, however, does not have to be that extreme. In a later chapter, we talk about the different ways we can be better matched. For now, let us examine how you can tell if you are in the wrong relationship.

Here are some warning signs:

- **If you have to make too many excuses for the person you are dating.**

  Do you constantly have to justify their behavior to family or friends? Do you make too many allowances for who they are fundamentally? Is age, occupation, family upbringing or relationship history problematic for you?

- **If you are trying to change him/her or he/she is trying to change you.**

  Everyone has the capacity and the desire to change. Most times, we want to improve certain aspects about ourselves that we know need to be adjusted. We want to be kinder, control our temper, be neater, more punctual and more like Jesus. But if that compulsion to change does not come from within and feels more like criticism and pressure to conform from your partner, that relationship is not ideal.

- **If they cause you to compromise who you are to be with them.**

  There is a measure of compromise required in every successful relationship. You will have to go shoe shopping with your future wife at some point in your relationship. He will ask you to sit through a Super Bowl and root for his favorite team. But, if she asks you to denounce a fundamental part of your core values, she is not for you. If he makes you compromise or jeopardize your walk with God, He is not for you.

- **If they are physically, verbally or emotionally abusive.**

  This point seems obvious to most people but those who stay in abusive relationships find it difficult to escape primarily due to fear. Fear of being alone, fear of being harmed in greater measure or fear for the safety of loved ones. I strongly caution you to seek outside assistance to help you break free from such relationships, if necessary. Do not be ashamed if you need help from the authorities, your pastor or family members to extract yourself from detrimental relationships. Your life may depend on it.

The first step to extracting yourself from a bad relationship is to end communication. You must refrain from calling, texting, scrolling social media, asking family members about them at least for a reasonable period of time, until you can interact with them in a mature, positive, healthy manner. If you never reach the point that you can carry on a conversation that does not hurt you or them, then communication has to cease indefinitely. If physically relocating is necessary for your safety and/or sanity, then move!

Secondly, I know it seems like a Christian cliché, but there is a lot to be said for fasting and prayer. As we discussed in the chapter about confusing sex with love, you can develop soul ties that are far more damaging to you than you realize. The only way to break those soul ties is through fasting and prayer. It also helps you heal completely when you add the spiritual component to the practical things that you do to overcome a break up.

Thirdly, working in the house of God is the absolute best answer to depression, loneliness and feelings of insignificance that often accompany ending a romantic relationship. Give yourself over to ministry. You should be doing that anyway! It causes you to take the focus off of yourself and minister to someone who is in worse condition than you. There is no better reward than the feeling of satisfaction that comes when you have met someone's need and changed someone's life for the better. It causes you to be grateful for your situation and circumstances. It makes you feel valued and valuable. It also heals your heart and your mind. There is something uniquely wonderful and therapeutic that God does when we begin to operate with the same sense of selflessness that Jesus did. It is all a part of the things that get *added* to you when you put the needs of the kingdom before your own.

Lastly, lean on your friends. This goes back to the importance of building a network of multiple, sound, healthy, godly friendships. Your friends will be there to get you out of your funk, take you out on an ice-cream date, cheer you up, buoy up your spirits and sustain you through the healing process. It is perfectly natural to be upset. Take the time to cry, vent, be angry and be hurt with the friend that you can trust not to betray your confidences. Let your friend, the prayer warrior, pray for you and speak life to you. Just do not stay in that place of bitterness or carry it to your next relationship. The best medicine for a broken heart is time but you do not have to spend your time wallowing. Instead, divert yourself with fun activities. Remember, the Bible tells us that weeping *may* come and stay for the night but joy is a definite promise on the horizon for you.

BASIC SOCIAL ETIQUETTE

The most common question that I have been asked is how to approach someone to whom you are attracted at church. We clearly recognize that the relationships formed at church, or better yet, in the kingdom require special handling. We know that there are "rules of engagement"; we just do not know precisely what they are. It is very apparent that we cannot treat God's sons and daughters like common people. Because of oversensitivity to this issue, often times, a simple hello, handshake or smile has been perceived as flirting. The Bible commands us to be a loving, kind, friendly people. I would caution you not to read too much in to what is a basic social custom.

There is nothing wrong with paying a member of the opposite sex a compliment as long as it is done in a tactful manner. We are created in the image of a God who loves praise. Wouldn't it stand to reason that we like to receive praise, too? A compliment is not a marriage proposal. It is not fair to assume someone paying you a compliment is flirting with you. Just accept the kind words for what they are, unless the person giving them is indicating that they mean something more.

If you find yourself attracted to a person of the opposite sex with whom you have had repeat contact, the best way to make those feelings known is to state clearly your desire to change the nature of your relationship. Keep in mind that you can be attracted but NOT "fulfill the lust of the flesh" based on those feelings. It is safer for a woman to wait until a man approaches her; however, I do not see the harm in a woman making the "first move" particularly if it is someone with whom you have a well-established friendship. I know some church cultures frown on women being the instigators of a relationship but that is not biblical. We use the scripture in Proverbs18:22 to justify making the men the only initiators in the relationship. Yes, "he that finds a wife finds a good thing", but that is more in reference to the condition in which he finds you. Prepare yourself to be a wife and he'll find you as wife. There is nothing that says wives cannot make it easy to be found.

If you are meeting someone or introducing yourself for the first time, just be yourself. The worst thing you can do is try to be what you THINK the other person wants. Keeping up the pretense over time can prove to be difficult. You be you, let them be them and see if you gel.

Here a few tips to consider when engaging in conversation:

◆ Avoid Elevator Eyes

- Do not leer at your brother or sister in Christ, looking them up and down in open appreciation.

◆ Wait for the Return Arrow

- Wait for the person to give you a clear signal it is ok to proceed with your advances or that they reciprocate your feelings of attraction.

◆ Be Sensitive

- Accept and/or provide rejection gracefully and tactfully. There is no need to humiliate someone who is expressing an attraction to you. There is no need to be angry with someone who does not reciprocate the attraction you have for them.

◆ Compliments do not include body parts

- "That suit is very becoming on you" is acceptable. "I sure love the way your biceps bulge in that t-shirt" is not!

◆ Do not use pet names

- Everyone does not readily acclimate to being called "Sweetie", "Honey" or "Baby" unless you have a well-established relationship. Be respectful. I love it when potential suitors call me Ms. Tyler. I also love it when that changes to a specified pet name that my suitor has for me once we have established relationship.

◆ Do not be readily/ easily offended

- If you have expressed interest in someone and they do not

return your affection, please do not take it personally. Maybe they are not attracted to you. It does not mean that you are not attractive to someone else. Maybe the timing is not right. Look at it from the perspective that the Lord may be saving you from potential harm or directing you to the person He has for you.

◆ Avoid Inappropriate touching

- I had to learn this one personally. I like to hug, touch people on the shoulder, or the arm when talking to them. Even though there was no sexual intent behind my actions, I have learned that certain gestures and touching can give the impression of flirting. I, like Rachel, am "well-favored" and I have an "anointing for hugs", so I had to learn to give members of the opposite sex that side hug that does not allow the "fullness of my glory to be revealed". I have some male friends that will put their hand on the small of my back to escort me through a door. That is fine for friends. I personally do not like it when people that I do not know well or especially the people I do not like touch me. Others may not either, so be careful.

I have also included an article listing the eight basic rules of etiquette everyone should follow on page 63 that may prove to be helpful.

SINGLE NOT ALONE

[SINGLE DEFINITION: NOT MARRIED; OF OR RELATED TO CELIBACY; A SEPARATE INDIVIDUAL OR THING; CONSISTING OF A SEPARATE, UNIQUE, WHOLE; UNACCOMPANIED BY OTHERS; EXCLUSIVELY ATTENTIVE; UNBROKEN , UNDIVIDED]

There seems to be a bit of a stigma, even in the church and among kingdom builders, that if you are single there is something wrong with you or that you must be lonely. Let me assure you, there is nothing wrong with you! You are not too tall, too fat, too skinny, too unattractive, too educated or too *you fill in the blank*. Your relationship status is not a deficiency, nor is it an indication that you are flawed beyond loving. Always, remember, you are fearfully and wonderfully made. You are loved beyond measure by a God who knows exactly what you need and how to give it to you.

I want to remind you, that you are single, not alone! Loneliness does not have to be your experience just because you are single. Do not let loneliness or the desire *not* to be alone, rush you into a relationship for which you are not ready. If the people in your circle are not satisfying your need for companionship, perhaps you need to expand your circle. Develop NEW hobbies and NEW interests so you can meet NEW people. Here are some statistics to consider when finding that special someone proves to be challenging:

♦ *There are 7.152 Billion people in the world.*

♦ *There are 103 Million unmarried people in the United States over the age of 18.*

♦ *There are 38 million people in California.*

♦ *There are 3.9 million people in Los Angeles.*

♦ *For every 100 unmarried women there are 87 unmarried men.*

♦ *62% of the unmarried U.S. residents have never been married. 24% were divorced and 14% were widowed.*

♦ *Approximately 23% of the adult unmarried population are people of color. Approximately 77% of the adult unmarried population is White.*

[ALONE DEFINITION:
1. ISOLATED, SOLITARY
2. SEPARATED FROM OTHERS
3. INCOMPARABLE, UNIQUE
4. LONELY, DESOLATE
5. WITHOUT AID OR SUPPORT
6. SOLELY, EXCLUSIVELY
7. CONSIDERED WITHOUT
REFERENCE TO ANY OTHER]

The feelings you attach to these definitions will determine what effect they will have on your season as a single person and who you will attract.

WHAT DOES IT MEAN TO BE EQUALLY YOKED?

II Corinthians 6:14 "Be ye not unequally yoked together with unbelievers: for what fellowship hath righteousness with unrighteousness? And what communion hath light with darkness?"

One of the greatest admonitions for the Christian single is not to be unequally yoked. It is often only used to describe a saved person not dating an unsaved person for obvious reasons; however, being equally yokes goes deeper than that. I often equate it to a three-legged race.

When you select a partner for a three-legged race you do not choose the person who will be the biggest hindrance to you crossing the finish line. You select someone who is about the same height or who is in good athletic condition and who can adapt and keep the same pace as you. You do not choose the person with a broken leg or who is drastically incompatible with you and then hope that you will win. You choose the person who is most likely to help you win. So, why would you choose a partner for something as significant as love and marriage who is not equipped to help get you over the finish line, saved or not?

When we talk about being equally yoked we are talking about compatibility in some of these areas: Spiritually, Personality, Financially, Physically, Emotionally/Psychologically, Sexually, Family, Education, Interests, Goals and Aspirations. Compatibility doesn't mean that you are exactly the same. It means that your traits complement one another and do not compete with one another. I have given just a few things to consider in each category. You may find other areas of your relationship in which to develop your compatibility. Nothing I say, however, overrides your discernment and being led by the Holy Spirit.

Spiritually

Do you have a compatible prayer life, study habit concerning God's Word, church attendance and service in the Kingdom? You should not only have a personal devotional habit, but devotional time that you share together. Have you been saved the same length of time?

Personality

Are your personalities compatible? Are you both talkative? Are you a morning person and she's a night owl? Is your sense of humor compatible? Are you an extravert and he's an introvert?

Financially

Are you both tithers? Do you give sacrificially at the same level? Are you both gainfully employed? Are your income levels well-matched? Do you both save and/ or invest? Are you thrifty and he's a shopaholic? Do you want to be financially independent? Do you have similar work ethics? Do you view money the same way?

Physically

You should be physically attracted to your spouse. Are you active and he's inactive? Do you share the same personal hygienic habits?

Emotionally/Psychologically

Make sure you are both healed from past relationships and that you have similar maturity levels. It is not wise to equate or compare your current relationship to other relationships. Do you have complementing temperaments?

Sexually

You should be sexually attracted to your spouse. You should know your future spouse's sexual history. Talk about your sexual appetites, frequency, preferences. When it comes to sensitive subjects like oral sex and anal sex, I would suggest you follow the guidelines as laid out by your spiritual leader if you have conviction over either. I am not suggesting that your pastor has control over your bedroom, but you want to please God in every area of your life including your sex life!

Family

Do you have similar family backgrounds? Carefully examine your future spouse's family, because they will be your family. Do you want a family together? Share your child-rearing views. If you both have children, prayerfully devise a plan for blending your families. Do you want to be a step-parent? Step-parenting is a whole other ballgame when you say "I do." Keep in mind that you have not raised that child from the time they were born and that interference from the other parent may be an obstacle with which you will have to deal. As much as is possible, try to develop relationship with the other parent. I would even suggest premarital family counseling with your future stepchildren.

Education

Are you similarly educated? Someone who hasn't finished high school may be intimidated by someone who holds a PhD. If your education levels are not matched, will that inspire you to further your own education or cause a rift in your relationship?

Interests

What do you like to do for fun outside of ministry? Do you like travel? Is he a sports fanatic? If you do not have similar recreational interests, will you feel excluded if your spouse indulges in a hobby that doesn't interest you? Is there something new you could both try together?

Goals and Aspirations

What kind of lifestyle do you want to live? What are your goals in ministry? Do you desire to be an entrepreneur? Do the goals and aspirations of your future spouse conflict with or coincide with yours?

Think about these and other areas of compatibility when deciding whether or not you are equally yoked with a partner. While you can improve in every area, if the motivation to change does not come from within, the change will not be permanent. If you go into a relationship expecting [THOU SHALT NOT PLOW WITH AN OX AND AN ASS. DEUTERONOMY 22:10] your partner to change and acclimate to your level of expectation in any of these areas, you can set yourself up for disappointment. Recognize that because you are both striving to please God, change will naturally take place, but it may not be the areas of change that you specifically want to see. Make sure you are happy with your partner "as is" so that when God matures him or her, your relationship is enhanced and you are both stronger for it.

Remember, you are selecting the best candidate to help you win, someone who will go the distance with you, not someone you have to train.

CONCLUSION

The greatest goal I have for writing this book and teaching this series is that you will gain better understanding of yourself and what you really desire in a spouse. I hope that you will really examine yourself, your relationships, who is connected to you and how your relationships are being used to build the kingdom of God. This part of the booklet contains a Love Language Test to help you define the ways you give and receive love. It is good to have your potential partner take the test, too, so you can understand how he or she gives and receives love. There is also a Personality Temperament Test that will give you a snapshot of your personality type. These assessments are not meant to box you in, but should be used merely as starting points to help you examine yourself.

There are also a few articles about etiquette, delaying gratification and abstinence to encourage you to elevate your thinking where sex before marriage is concerned. I recognize that the struggle to refrain from sexual activity can sometimes be overwhelming, to say the least. I also know that we can win! If we retrain and transform our minds and the spirit of our minds, we can retrain our habits and curb our desires. I pray that the information contained in this book will help you build lasting relationships and ultimately a marriage that exemplifies and glorifies God.

...Be not conformed to this world: but be ye transformed by the renewing of your mind...Romans 12:22

That ye put off concerning the former conversation the old man, which is corrupt according to the deceitful lusts; And be renewed in the spirit of your mind. Ephesians 4:22-23

SUPPLEMENTAL MATERIAL

This portion of the booklet contains the **Love Language Quiz** as established by Dr. Gary Chapman in his book *"The 5 Love Languages"*, originally published by Northfield Publishing in 1995,

The **Personality Temperament Test** as established by Tim LaHaye in his book "Why You Act the Way You Do" published by Tyndale Momentum, May 26, 1988.

The following articles are also included in this portion of the booklet:
8 Basic Etiquette Rules that Everyone Should Follow
By Becky Smith, Yahoo.com

Sexual Atheism: Christian Dating Data Reveals a Deeper Spiritual Malaise Published April 10, 2014 by Kenny Luck on ChristianPost.com

The Power of Delaying Gratification-How to develop impulse control Published on July 29, 2012 by Alex Lickerman, M.D. in Happiness in this World

Delay of Gratification and Exceptional Marriages
Published on March 23, 2013 by Dr. Shauna H. Springer in The Joint (Ad) Ventures of Well-Educated Couples

Works Cited
Franz, Gordon. www.Biblearchaeology.org. 12 June 2013. 19 March 2015
        <www.Biblearchaeology.org>.
Wikipedia. 10 January 2001. 16 March 2015 <http://en.wikipedia.org/wiki/Courtship>.

LOVE LANGUAGE QUIZ

For each pair of the following statements, circle the one that fits you best within your relationship. If you are not currently in a relationship, try to imagine how you would like to be treated if you were. Or think about how you like to be treated by family members and close friends.

1. I like to receive encouraging or affirming notes **A**
I like to be hugged **E**

2. I like to spend one-to-one time with close friends **B**
I feel loved when someone gives me practical help **D**

3. I like it when people give me gifts **C**
I like leisurely visits with friends and loved ones **B**

4. I feel loved when people do things to help me **D**
I feel loved when people give me a reassuring hand shake or hug **E**

5. I feel loved when someone I love or admire puts their arm around me **E**
I feel loved when I receive a gift from someone I admire or love **C**

6. I like to go places with friends or loved ones **B**
I like to high-five or slap around with friends who are special to me **E**

7. Visible symbols of love (such as gifts) are important to me **C**
I feel loved when people affirm me **A**

8. I like to sit close to people I enjoy being around **E**
I like it when people tell me I'm attractive/handsome **A**

9. I like to spend time with friends and loved ones **B**
I like to receive little gifts from friends and loved ones **C**

10. Words of acceptance are important to me **A**
I know someone loves me when he or she helps me **D**

11. I like being together and doing things with friends & loved ones **B**
I like it when kind words are spoken to me **A**

12. What someone does affects me far more than what they say **D**
Hugs make me feel connected and valued **E**

13. I value praise and try to avoid criticism **A**
Several small gifts mean more to me than one large gift **C**

14. I feel close to someone when we are talking or doing something together **B**
I feel closer to friends & loved ones when we wrestle, hug or shake hands **E**

15. I like for people to compliment my achievements **A**
I know people love me when they do things for me they do not enjoy doing **D**

16. I like for people to cross the street to shake hands or hug when they see me **E**
I like when people listen to me & show genuine interest in what I'm saying **B**

17. I feel loved when friends and loved ones help me with jobs or projects **D**

I really enjoy receiving gifts from friends and loved ones **C**

18. I like for people to compliment my appearance **A**
I feel loved when people take time to understand my feelings **B**

19. I feel secure when a special person is physically close to me **E**
Acts of service make me feel loved **D**

20. I appreciate the many things that special people do for me **D**
I like to receive gifts that special people make for me **C**

21. I really enjoy the feeling I get when someone gives me undivided attention **B**
I really enjoy the feeling I get when someone does some act to serve me **D**

22. I feel loved when a person celebrates my birthday with a gift **C**
I feel loved when a person celebrates my birthday with meaningful words **A**

23. I know a person is thinking of me when they give me a gift **C**
I feel loved when a person helps me with my chores or tasks **D**

24. I appreciate it when someone listens patiently and doesn't interrupt me **B**
I appreciate it when someone remembers special days with a gift **C**

25. I like knowing loved ones are concern enough to help with my daily tasks **D**
I enjoy extended trips with someone who is special to me **B**

26. I do not mind the "kiss-hello" with friends I am close to **E**
Receiving a gift given for no special reason excites me **C**

27. I like to be told that I am appreciated **A**
I like for a person to look at me when they are talking **B**

28. Gifts from a friend or loved one are always special to me **C**
I feel good when a friend or loved one hugs or touches me **E**

29. I feel loved when a person enthusiastically does some task I have requested **D**
I feel loved when I am told how much I am appreciated **A**

30. I need physical contact with people every day **E**
I need words of encouragement and affirmation everyday **A**

Now go through your quiz again and count how many "A, B, C, D and Es" you circled and place the number in below.

TOTALS:
A: _____ B: _____ C: _____ D: _____ E: _____

Which letter has your highest score? That is your *primary* love language. Recognize that we give and receive love using all of the love languages but there are some that are stronger than others:

•A = Words of Affirmation •D = Acts of Service
•B = Quality Time   •E = Physical Touch
•C = Receiving Gifts

8 BASIC ETIQUETTE RULES THAT EVERYONE SHOULD FOLLOW *BY BECKY SMITH, YAHOO.COM*

Even as this article is being written there is a cell phone ringing in a church or a movie theater. Someone is probably talking with their mouth full or chewing gum while they take your food order.

In today's fast paced world it is easy to forget some of the common courtesies that should be basic and non-negotiable. Unfortunately, many people appear to have forgotten the manners that were taught to them by their parents and grandparents and sadly, others do not appear to have ever been taught any manners at all.

It is not hard to behave in a socially correct way; however, the masses seem to think that having a bit of decorum is "old fashioned" or "boring". Obviously, this is not true. If people would just take a few moments to review the basic rules of good etiquette they would find that it would help them not only in their personal lives, but in their business relationships as well.

Outlined below are protocols that will help to refine the social graces and improve the impression that others have of you.

Basic Politeness. Showing politeness is not difficult. It is simple to say "please", "thank you", "you are welcome", and "excuse me". These phrases show that a person is considerate of others. Even if someone is rude, and not your favorite person it is better to be polite to them rather than sinking to their level.

Men, Remove Your Hat Indoors. Most young men of today do not even seem to be aware of the fact that it is considered rude to wear a hat (mostly ball caps these days) indoors. Gentlemen, when you enter a building please remove hats and caps.

Hold That Door. This is a rule that does not just apply to men anymore. Yes, men should still hold the door for ladies and allow them to enter or exit first, but ladies are not exempt from holding the door for their elders or someone who might have their hands full. And while it might seem an outdated notion, nothing says "gentleman" like going around to the passenger side to open the car door for a lady.

Be On Time. There is nothing worse than to be kept waiting and if you are the offending party who is late, it is just rude. If you tend to always run late, set your clocks ahead 10 or 15 minutes so that you will arrive on time.

Do Not Groom Yourself In Public. If you have something that needs picking, scratching, combing, or any other form of grooming, please do not do it in mixed company. Take your personal needs to the restroom or wait until you get home. Ladies, it is okay to quickly and discretely apply a little lipstick without using a mirror. It is not, however, okay to pull out a compact and a suitcase full of cosmetics and start redoing your face. Also, please refrain from clipping and filing your nails in public. This is unbelievably crude.

Keep Gum Chewing To A Minimum. If you must chew gum for a legitimate reason such as having bad breath or dry mouth, try to do it in your car between stops. If it is absolutely necessary to chew gum in a public place, please do not smack it, chomp it, or blow bubbles with it.

Turn The Ringer Off. When entering any public establishment the first thing you should do is set your cell phone to vibrate. Remember you do not have to answer every call, that is what voice mail is for. If you know that it is a call of importance, excuse yourself and move to the lobby or another room to take the call. Keep the call time short and let your caller know that you will return their call at your earliest convenience.

Keep The Conversation Polite. When engaging in conversation, whether it is at work, or in a more social setting, never bring up money, religion, or politics. These subjects are a powder keg waiting to explode, and while we are on the subject of exploding, please refrain from speaking loudly, yelling, or using profanity.

Simply put, good manners are a sign that you have consideration for others and extending these common courtesies shows that you have class and good breeding.

SEXUAL ATHEISM: CHRISTIAN DATING DATA REVEALS A DEEPER SPIRITUAL MALAISE

Published April 10, 2014 by <u>Kenny Luck</u> on <u>ChristianPost.com</u>

The guy sitting across from me is a professing and practicing Christian. He drops by my office unannounced today to talk to me about his new online dating life. Specifically, he wants to talk about the over-willingness of Christian women he has encountered on several of his dates who want to jump right from a very public conversation and vanilla latte at Starbucks to very private whispers and physical exchanges between the sheets back at his place.

Usually this gender scenario is reversed, but the sex, love and dating landscape continues to move in a progressively liberal direction among Christians without any solid indicators that it will change anytime soon. Both sexes today, across all ages and Christian demographics, are prone to compartmentalize their faith away from their sexual life.

While Christian singles report praying and church attendance are highly desirable qualities in the dating matrix, a troubling and confusing dichotomy arises when the issue of sex before marriage presents itself. Specifically, single Christians enter a sexual fog. That fog clouds and hides the reality that an identity rooted in Christ should manifest itself in intelligent and hope-filled sexual restraint based on God's promises and instead replaces it with fear and pride-filled choices based on some other promise they believe more.

In a recent study conducted by ChristianMingle.com, Christian singles between the ages of 18 to 59 were asked, "Would you have sex before marriage?" The response? Sixty-three percent of the single Christian respondents indicated yes. The guy sitting across from me is a professing and practicing Christian. He drops by my office unannounced today to talk to me about his new online dating life. Specifically, he wants to talk about the over-willingness of Christian women he has encountered on several of his dates who want to jump right from a very public conversation and vanilla latte at Starbucks to very private whispers and physical exchanges between the sheets back at his place.

It is equally honest to say that nearly nine out of 10 self-proclaimed single Christians are, in practice, sexual atheists. In other words, God has nothing to say to them on that subject of any consequence or, at least, anything meaningful enough to dissuade them from following their own course of conduct. It is the ultimate oxymoron. A person who at once believes in a wise, sovereign and loving God who created them and all things, can also believe simultaneously He should not, cannot or will not inform their thinking or living sexually. It reminds me of those famous red letters in Luke's Gospel where Jesus says, "Why do you call me 'Lord, Lord' and do not do what I say?" (Luke 6:46, NIV). There is disconnect between identity and activity.

If you let the paint mentally dry on the statistic above and the perception about God it reflects for a moment, perhaps my contention of sexual atheism won't seem so far-fetched. No amount of hand-wringing at the many-headed hydra of the entertainment world or raucous deploring of immoral political philosophies invading our nation can explain this one.

No, our life in God and for our God reflects our real view of God. These are our adults who populate our weekend services, attend our Bible studies, download our podcast messages, pray often and who have Jesus Culture, TobyMac and Maroon 5 in their playlists. Having tracked this trend among youth for decades, it is no surprise to me that the broad spectrum of single adults—yesterday's youth—both feel and act this way. We should really make an effort to not be too shocked or surprised.

Jesus Himself said it would trend this way. The apostle Paul forewarned the very single, very godly Timothy that there would be times in his ministry when clear and sound doctrine in Scripture would be defeated by broken culture teaming up with the ever-present and self-serving nature within every Christian. He accurately forecasted a self-styled Christianity that reflected culture over the character of Christ in personal moral spaces and practice. And nothing, from any frame of reference, is more personal and more moral than our choices regarding sexual expression. It is where the spiritual rubber really hits the road. But interestingly, Paul's counsel to Timothy for that time when he saw these trends manifesting on a grand scale was this: "Be serious about everything, endure hardship, do the work of an evangelist, fulfill your ministry" (2 Tim. 4:5, HCSB). Solid, timely and reliable advice like this was needed then and is really needed now.

As God's men and women, as fathers and mothers, as pastors and lay ministers and as loving brothers and sisters, we too must keep our heads clear. We must do our work in the midst of this attack on the body of Christ and fulfill our ministries in the midst of this spiritual battle. We must faithfully and directly speak into the relevant spiritual and practical themes that are at the root of the issue instead of wasting our time bemoaning the symptoms these statistics represent. We must graciously but prophetically call out the shortsightedness of Christians who are borrowing trouble sexually and sinning against God and others in the process through our messaging and ministries. We must confront ourselves and our brothers and sisters with the veracity, authority and loving transparency of Scripture, which reflects God's love and wisdom in life-saving and marriage-saving ways. That is, we must point out the truth that if I am undisciplined sexually before marriage and willing to compromise my convictions before marriage, a wedding ring will not make me disciplined after marriage. But most importantly and practically, we must avail ourselves of the ministries, tools and resources that are speaking into this clearly massive hole of spiritual life and practice among our single brothers and sisters.

The love, sex and dating forecast among adult single believers for the foreseeable future is this: cloudy with a chance of fear and pride. Instead of believing that God knows better, Christian adults will believe they know how to meet their needs better or, on the more arrogant end, that they know better when it comes to sex and dating, period.

To say that professing or self-described Christians are becoming more liberal means that their reference point for assessing and practicing sexuality is more cultural and personal rather than biblical or spiritual. It means that they possess a low view of God and Scripture and a high view of self and culture as the key drivers of their moral and sexual behavior.

Practical sexual atheism among Christians says God can speak into some things but not sex. This ultimate expression of self-deception and loss of mind goes all the way back to the garden, when a certain character asked Adam and Eve: "Did God really say that?" They took the bait and, apparently, so are the majority of single Christians in the garden of love, sex and dating. They are listening to the voice that says, "Eat and have your eyes opened." Like the first couple, God's single men and women are letting fear win over faith and curiosity win over Christ with inevitable and untold prices to pay.

But it is not a time to act high and mighty. It is time to act graciously but truthfully with our single brothers and sisters. For they, along with us, will have that moment in front of the living Christ, and we want that moment to be the best it can possibly be. To realize such an epic and eternal moment, we not only have to pray for them, but we also have to equip them practically with the best possible teachings and tools that serve to restore a vision of God that transforms them in their context.

We have to engage the culture, not run.

THE POWER OF DELAYING GRATIFICATION: HOW TO DEVELOP IMPULSE CONTROL

Published on July 29, 2012 by <u>Alex Lickerman, M.D.</u> in <u>Happiness in this World</u>

In 1970 psychologist Walter Mischel famously placed a cookie in front of a group of children and gave them a choice: they could eat the cookie immediately, or they could wait until he returned from a brief errand and then be rewarded with a second. If they didn't wait, however, they'd be allowed to eat only the first one. Not surprisingly, once he left the room, many children ate the cookie almost immediately. A few, though, resisted eating the first cookie long enough to receive the second. Mischel termed these children *high-delay children*.

Interestingly, the children who were best able to delay gratification subsequently did better in school and had fewer behavioral problems than the children who could only resist eating the cookie for a few minutes—and, further, ended up on average with SAT scores that were 210 points higher. As adults, the high-delay children completed college at higher rates than the other children and then went on to earn higher incomes. In contrast, the children who had the most trouble delaying gratification had higher rates of incarceration as adults and were more likely to struggle with drug and alcohol <u>addiction</u>.

Which all suggests that the ability to delay gratification—that is, impulse control—may be one of the most important skills to learn to have a satisfying and successful life. The question is how do we learn it? The answer may lie in the strategies Mischel's high-delay children used. Rather than resist the urge to eat the cookie, these children *distracted* themselves from the urge itself. They played with toys in the room, sang songs to themselves, and looked everywhere but at the cookie. In short, they did everything they could to put the cookie out of their minds.

Taking his cue from these high-delay children, in a <u>second study</u>, Mischel placed two marshmallows side by side in front of a different group of children to whom he explained, as in the previous study, that eating the first before he returned to the room would mean they couldn't eat the second. He then instructed one group of them to imagine when he stepped out of the room how much marshmallows are like clouds: round, white, and puffy. (He instructed a control group, in contrast, to imagine how sweet and chewy and soft they were.) A third group he instructed to visualize the crunchiness and saltiness of pretzels. Perhaps not surprisingly, the children who visualized the qualities of the marshmallows that were unrelated to eating them (that is, the way in which they were similar to clouds) waited almost three times longer than children who were instructed to visualize how delicious the marshmallows would taste. Most intriguing, however, was that picturing the pleasure of eating pretzels produced the longest delay in gratification of all. Apparently, imagining the pleasure they'd feel from indulging in an unavailable temptation distracted the children even more than cognitively restructuring the way they thought about the temptation before them.

In other words, one of the most effective ways to distract ourselves from a tempting pleasure we do not want to indulge is by focusing on *another pleasure*. So the next time you find yourself confronted with a temptation—whether a piece of cake, a drink of alcohol, or a psychoactive drug—do not employ willpower to resist it. Send your attention somewhere else by imagining a different pleasure not immediately available to you. For if you can successfully turn your attention elsewhere until the temptation is removed from your environment or you remove yourself from its environment, the odds that you'll give in to your impulse will decrease more than with almost any other intervention you can try.

DELAY OF GRATIFICATION
AND EXCEPTIONAL MARRIAGES

Delaying gratification is linked to happy, long-lasting marriages
Published on March 23, 2013 by Dr. Shauna H. Springer in The Joint
(Ad) Ventures of Well-Educated Couples
Become a "Two-Marshmallow" Person

Making conscious choices that allow you to live in alignment with your deepest values often requires the ability to delay gratification. In the 1960s, Stanford University researcher Walter Mischel came up with an elegantly simple method that showed the value of the ability to delay gratification. His study subjects were a group of four-year-old children.

Mischel offered each participant a large, puffy marshmallow but told them all that if they would wait for him to run an errand, they could have not one, but two, lovely marshmallows. The marshmallow was an excellent choice because it had not only the taste, but also the appearance and texture of a delectable treat. The little tykes squirmed in front of their marshmallows like dogs might whimper when told to stay while sitting in front of T-bone steaks dripping with meaty juices.

Some of the four-year-olds were able to control their impulse to snatch up and consume their marshmallows for the duration of Mischel's 15–20-minute errand (which must have felt like several lifetimes for these four-year-olds). Others could not.

Mischel followed up with his subjects many years later and found that the ability to control impulses and delay gratification was associated with success in many different areas of life as an adult. For instance, those who delayed gratification were more self-motivated and more persistent in the face of obstacles. On average, they scored 210 points higher on SAT tests. Those who had quickly consumed the first marshmallow they were offered continued to have <u>impulse-control</u> problems in adulthood. Mischel characterized them as more troubled, stubborn, indecisive, and mistrustful, and less self-confident.

When you have done the work of clarifying your values, it is important to think long-term in setting up your life. For example, instead of pursuing work that pays well now but has no intrinsic reward or personal growth potential, consider investing the time and energy to gain skills that will flower into a stimulating work life for the rest of your <u>career</u>.

When you take the long view of your life, it makes the most sense to become a two-marshmallow person, especially where your deepest values are concerned. Moreover, the traits that line up with good character (patience, self-control, discernment, long-term thinking style) have significant overlap with those that Mischel captured and elucidated in his landmark study.

Being a "two marshmallow" person is critical in the area of long-term satisfying relationships. An exceptional <u>marriage</u> is often the result of the union between two individuals who enter the marriage with good character and who continue to shape each other's character in positive ways over time.

I would argue that most of the things that are worth achieving in life require us to delay gratification and to prioritize restraint over indulgence in more primitive drives. The discipline of being a two-marshmallow person can pay off in many ways as you create an interesting life with a well-matched two-marshmallow partner. During the dating phase of a relationship, waiting for a partner who is capable of maintaining a lifelong, happy marriage, and enjoying a long courtship with that person to really test mutual compatibility is an adult version of waiting for two marshmallows.

In fact, the question is actually this: Are you willing to wait for a lifelong supply of lovely marshmallows that flow from an exceptional marriage, or do you want to bite down, right now, on something that resembles a marshmallow but may well turn into a bag of pus once you've committed? (I wonder if this explains why the Spanish word *esposas* means both "wives" and "handcuffs".)

PERSONALITY TEMPERAMENT TEST

INSTRUCTIONS: This is a Personality Temperament Test taken from Tim LaHaye's book, "Why You Act the Way You Do". It helps assess your temperament of potential strengths & weaknesses. It is very simple and takes about 45 minutes to complete. There are 4 Sections below. In each section you will find a series of descriptive words. Your job is to read each word and put a number next to it according to how well it describes the REAL you. After you have completed all 4 Sections go to page 2 for further instructions. To get a more accurate assessment of your temperament have 3-4 close friends &/or family members also complete a test about your temperament.

REMEMBER: It is important that you be honest and objective. Do not mark a box according to how you want to be seen; rather mark it according to how you really are. If it is NATURALLY who you are then it isn't something that you are "working on" nor is it something that requires a lot of effort in order for you to be that way. It just comes naturally. Some of the descriptive words below are very flattering words and some are unflattering words. Do not answer according to how you want to be or do not want to be. BE COMPLETELY 100% HONEST WITH YOURSELF....

SCORING CRITERIA: Score how each word best describes			
1 = "That is definitely NOT		**2 =** "That is usually NOT	
3 = "That is usually me."		**4 =** "That is mostly me."	
		5 = "That IS definitely me!"	

Section 1	Section 2	Section 3	Section 4
__ emotional	__ optimistic	__ deep feeling	__ very quiet
__ egotistical	__ determined	__ critical	__ selfish
__ interrupts others	__ bossy	__ insecure	__ unenthusiastic
__ compassionate	__ goal-oriented	__ sensitive	__ negative
__ impulsive	__ decisive	__ indecisive	__ regular daily
__ disorganized	__ frank	__ hard to please	habits
__ impractical	__ self-confident	__ self-centered	__ hesitant
__ funny	__ sarcastic	__ pessimistic	__ shy
__ forgetful	__ workaholic	__ depressed	__ stingy
__ easily discouraged	__ self-sufficient	__ easily	__ aimless
__ very positive	__ practical	__ easily offended	__ not aggressive
__ easily angered	__ headstrong	__ idealistic	__ stubborn
__ undisciplined	__ activist	__ loner	__ worrier
__ extrovert	__ outgoing	__ self-sacrificing	__ spectator of
__ refreshing	__ domineering	__ introvert	life
__ lively/spirited	__ adventurous	__ faithful friend	__ works wel
__ weak-willed	__ aggressive	__ analytical	under pressure
__ spontaneous	__ competitive	__ considerate	__ indecisive
__ talkative	__ leadership	__ likes behind the	__ adaptable
__ delightful/cheerful	ability	scenes	__ slow and lazy
__ enjoyable	__ daring	__ suspicious	__ submissive to
__ popular	__ persevering	__ respectful	others
__ friendly/sociable	__ bold	__ introspective	__ easy going
__ "bouncy"	__ strong-willed	__ planner	__ reserved
__ restless	__ persuasive	__ perfectionist	__ calm and cool
__ difficulty	__ hot-tempered	__ scheduled	__ content/
concentrating	__ resourceful	__ unforgiving	satisfied
__ likes to play	__ insensitive	/resents	__ efficient
__ difficulty keeping	__ outspoken	__ orderly	__ patient
resolutions	__ unsympathetic	__ creative	__ dependable
__ lives in present	__ productive	__ detailed	__ listener
__ difficulty with		__ moody	__ witty/dry
appointments		__ gifted (musically	humor
		or athletically)	__ pleasant
			__ teases others
			__ consistent

ONCE YOU HAVE COMPLETED ALL 4 SECTIONS...

After you have completed all 4 Sections go back and cancel out each description that you scored either a 1 or 2 by drawing a line through that number. Since that score is so low it, doesn't really apply to your overall scoring in each Section. Now add up all of the 3's, 4's & 5's in each Section and write your total at the bottom of each appropriate section. The section with the highest score is your Primary Temperament and the section with the second highest score is your Secondary Temperament. No one is one pure temperament, but instead we are a blend of all the temperaments.

WHAT'S MY PERSONALITY TEMPERAMENT?

Each section represents one of four Temperaments:

SECTION 1: Sanguine Temperament

(Fun-loving extrovert; outgoing; very social; "the life of the party") – EXTROVERT

SECTION 2: Choleric Temperament

(Focused; extrovert; goal oriented; "the achiever") - EXTROVERT

SECTION 3: Melancholy Temperament (detailed; introspective; artistic; "the naturally gifted") - INTROVERT

SECTION 4: Phlegmatic Temperament

(Easy going; stable; consistent; "the loyal friend") - INTROVERT

WHAT'S MY PERSONALITY TEMPERAMENT BLEND?

Since everyone is a combination of the four Temperaments you need to find out what your Temperament "Blend" is by assessing what your Primary & Secondary Temperaments are. The section with the highest score is your Primary Temperament and the section with the second highest score is your Secondary Temperament. Now morph your Primary & Secondary together. In other words, if you scored highest in Section 2 (Choleric) and second highest in Section 4 (Phlegmatic) then your Temperament Blend would be "ChlorPhleg". Or if you scored highest in Section 1 (Sanguine) and second highest in Section 3 (Melancholy) then your Temperament Blend would be "SanMel". If you tied in any Section then see which Section had the most 5's to determine which Section more accurately represents you. It is also possible to be a Tri-Blend Temperament who has 3 dominant Temperaments.

WHAT'S MY PERSONALITY TEMPERAMENT PROFILE?

Once you have figured out your Temperament Blend it is time to read about your Temperament Profile to see what some of your potential strengths and some of your potential weaknesses are, as well as to find out what Bible character might have displayed a similar Temperament. Read the next few pages to get a snapshot of your Temperament Blend.

It is very important to realize that this is just a snapshot of your temperament blend.

THE 12 BLENDS OF TEMPERAMENTS

The SanChlor

The strongest extrovert of all the blends of temperaments will be the SanChlor, for the two temperaments that make up his nature are both extroverted. The happy charisma of the sanguine makes him a people-oriented, enthusiastic, salesman type; but the choleric side of his nature will provide him with the necessary resolution and character traits that will fashion a somewhat more organized and productive individual than if he were pure sanguine. Almost any people-oriented field is open to him, but to sustain his interest it must offer variety, activity, and excitement.

The potential weaknesses of a SanChlor are usually apparent to everyone because he is such an external person. He customarily talks too much, thus exposing himself and his weaknesses for all to see. He is highly opinionated. Consequently, he expresses himself loudly even before he knows all the facts. To be honest, no one has more mouth trouble! If he is the life of the party, he is lovable; but if he feels threatened or insecure, he can become obnoxious. His leading emotional problem will be anger, which can catapult him into action at the slightest provocation. Since he combines the easy forgetfulness of the sanguine and the stubborn casuistry of the choleric, he may not have a very active conscience. Consequently, he tends to justify his actions. This man, like any other temperament, needs to be filled daily with the Holy Spirit and the Word of God.

Simon Peter, the self-appointed leader of the twelve apostles, is a classic example of a New Testament Sandlot. He obviously had mouth trouble, demonstrating this repeatedly by speaking up before anyone else could. He talked more in the Gospels than all the others put together - and most of what he said was wrong. He was egotistical, weak-willed, and carnal throughout the Gospels. In Acts, however, he was a remarkably transformed man - resolute, effective, and productive. What made the difference? He was filled with the Spirit.

The SanMel

SanMels are highly emotional people who fluctuate drastically. They can laugh hysterically one minute and burst into tears the next. It is almost impossible for them to hear a sad tale, observe a tragic plight of another person, or listen to melancholic music without weeping profusely. They genuinely feel the grief's of others. Almost any field is open to them, especially public speaking, acting, music, and the fine arts. However, SanMels reflect an uninhibited perfectionism that often alienates them from others because they verbalize their criticisms. They are usually people-oriented individuals who have sufficient substance to make a contribution to other lives - if their ego and arrogance do not make them so obnoxious that others become hostile to them.

One of the crucial weaknesses of this temperament blend prevails in SanMel's thought-life. Both sanguines and melancholies are dreamers, and thus if the melancholy part of his nature suggests a negative train of thought, it can nullify a SanMel's potential. It is easy for him to get down on himself. In addition, this person, more than most others, will have both an anger problem and a tendency toward fear. Both temperaments in his makeup suffer with an insecurity problem; not uncommonly, he is fearful to utilize his potential. Being admired by others is so important to him that it will drive him to a consistent level of performance. He has a great ability to commune with God, and if he walks in the Spirit he will make an effective servant of Christ.

King David is a classic illustration of the SanMel temperament. An extremely likable man who attracted both men and women; he was colorful, dramatic, emotional and weak-willed. He could play a harp and sing, he clearly demonstrated a poetic instinct in his Psalms, and he made decisions on impulse. Unfortunately, like many SanMels, he fouled up his life by a series of disastrous and costly mistakes before he gained enough self-discipline to finish out his destiny. All SanMels, of course, are not able to pick up the pieces of their lives and start over as David did. It is far better for them to walk in the Spirit daily and avoid such mistakes.

The SanPhleg

The easiest person to like is a SanPhleg. The overpowering and obnoxious tendencies of a sanguine are offset by the gracious, easygoing phlegmatic. SanPhlegs are extremely happy people who carefree spirit and good humor make them lighthearted entertainers sought after by others. Helping people is their regular business, along with sales of various kinds. They are the least extroverted of any of the sanguines and are often regulated by their environment and circumstances rather than being self-motivated. SanPhlegs are naturally pro-family and preserve the love of their children - and everyone else for that matter. They would not purposely hurt anyone. The SanPhleg's greatest weaknesses are lack of motivation and discipline. He would rather socialize than work, and he tends to take life to   4 casually. As an executive remarked about one, "He is the nicest guy I ever fired." He rarely gets upset over anything and tends to find the bright side of everything. He usually has an endless repertoire of jokes and delights in making others laugh, often when the occasion calls for seriousness. When Jesus Christ becomes the chief object of his love, he is transformed into a more resolute, purposeful, and productive person.

The first-century evangelist Apollos is about as close as we can come to a New Testament illustration of the SanPhleg. A skilled orator who succeeded Paul and other who had founded the churches, he did the work of stirring the churches with his Spirit-filled preaching and teaching. Loved by all, followed devotedly by some, this pleasant and dedicated man apparently traveled a great deal but did not found new works.

The ChlorSan

The second-strongest extrovert among the blends of temperament will be the reverse of the first - the ChlorSan. This man's life is given over completely to activity. Most of his efforts are productive and purposeful, but watch his recreation - it is so activity-prone that it borders being violent. He is a natural promoter and salesman, with enough charisma to get along well with others. Certainly the best motivator of people and one who thrives on a challenge, he is almost fearless and exhibits boundless energy. His wife will often comment, "He has only two speeds, wide open and stop." Mr. ChlorSan is the courtroom attorney who can charm the coldest-hearted judge and jury, the fund-raiser who can get people to contribute what they intended to save, the man who never goes anywhere unnoticed, the preacher who combines both practical Bible teaching and church administration, and the politician who talks his state into changing its constitution so he can represent them one more time. A convincing debater, what he lacks in facts or arguments he makes up in bluff or bravado. As a teacher, he is an excellent communicator,   particularly in the social sciences; rarely is he drawn to math, science, or the abstract. Whatever his professional occupation, his brain is always in motion.

The weaknesses of this man, the chief of which is hostility, are as broad as his talents. He combines the quick, explosive anger of the sanguine (without the forgiveness) and the long-burning resentment of the choleric. He is the one personality type who not only gets ulcers himself, but gives them to others. Impatient with those who do not share his motivation and energy, he prides himself on being brutally frank (some call it sarcastically frank). It is difficult for him to concentrate on one thing very long, which is why he often enlists others to finish what he has started. He is opinionated, prejudiced, impetuous, and inclined doggedly to finish a project he probably should not have started in the first place. If not controlled by God, he is apt to justify anything he does - and rarely hesitates to manipulate or walk over other people to accomplish his ends. Most ChlorSans get so engrossed in their work that they neglect wife and family, even lashing out at them if they complain. Once he comprehends the importance of giving love and approval to his family, however, he can transform his entire household.

James, the author of the biblical book that bears his name, could well have been a ChlorSan - at least his book sounds like it. The main thrust of the book declares that "faith without works is dead" - a favored concept of work-loving cholerics. He used the practical and logical reasoning of a choleric, yet was obviously a highly esteemed man of God. On human weakness he discusses - the fire of the tongue and how no man can control it (James 3) - relates directly to this temperament's most vulnerable characteristic, for we all know the ChlorSans feature a razor-sharp, active tongue. His victory and evident productiveness in the cause of Christ is a significant example to any thoughtful ChlorSan.

The ChlorMel

The choleric/melancholy is an extremely industrious and capable person. The optimism and practicality of the choleric overcome the tendency toward moodiness of the melancholy, making the ChlorMel both goal-oriented and detailed. Such a person usually does well in school, possesses a quick, analytical mind, and yet is decisive. He develops into a thorough leader, the kind whom one can always count on to do an extraordinary job. Never take him on in a debate unless you are assured of your facts, for he will make mincemeat of you, combining verbal aggressiveness and attention to detail. This man is extremely competitive and forceful in all that he does. He is a dogged researcher and is usually successful, no matter what kind of business he pursues. This temperament probably makes the best natural leader. General George S. Patton, the great commander of the U.S. Third Army in World War II who drove the German forces back to Berlin, was probably a ChlorMel.

Equally as great as his strengths, are his weaknesses. He is apt to be autocratic, a dictator type who inspires admiration and hate simultaneously. He is usually a quick-witted talker whose sarcasm can devastate others. He is a natural-born crusader whose work habits are irregular and long. A ChlorMel harbors considerable hostility and resentment, and unless he enjoys a good love relationship with his parents, he will find interpersonal relationships difficult, particularly with his family. No man is more apt to be an overly strict disciplinarian than the ChlorMel father. He combines the hard-to-please tendency of the choleric and the perfectionism of the melancholy. When controlled by the Holy Spirit, however, his entire emotional life is transformed and he makes an outstanding Christian.

There is little doubt in my mind that the Apostle Paul was a ChlorMel. Before his conversion he was hostile and cruel, for the Scripture teaches that he spent his time persecuting and jailing Christians. Even after his conversion, his strong-willed determination turned to unreasonable bullheadedness, as when he went up to Jerusalem against the will and warning of God. His writings and ministry demonstrate the combination of the practical-analytical reasoning and the self-sacrificing but extremely driving nature of a ChlorMel. He is a good example of God's transforming power in the life of a ChlorMel who is completely dedicated to God's will.

The ChlorPhleg

The most subdued of all the extrovert temperaments is the ChlorPhleg, a happy blend of the quick, active, and hot with the calm, cool, and unexcited. He is not as apt to rush into things as quickly as the preceding extroverts because he is more deliberate and subdued. He is extremely capable in the long run, although he does not particularly impress you that way at first. He is a very organized person who combines planning and hard work. People usually enjoy working with and for him because he knows where he is going and has charted his course, yet is not unduly severe with people. He has the ability to help others make the best use of theirs skills and rarely offends people or makes them feel used. The ChlorPhleg's slogan on organization states: "Anything that needs to be done can be done better if it is organized." These men are usually good husbands and fathers as well as excellent administrators in almost any field.

In spite of his obvious capabilities, the ChlorPhleg is not without a notable set of weaknesses. Although not as addicted to the quick anger of some temperaments, he is known to harbor resentment and bitterness. Some of the cutting edge of choleric's sarcasm is here offset by the gracious spirit of the phlegmatic; so instead of uttering cutting and cruel remarks, his barbs are more apt to emerge as cleverly disguised humor. One is never quite sure whether he is kidding or ridiculing, depending on his mood. No one can be more bull headedly stubborn that a ChlorPhleg and it is very difficult for him to change his mind once it is committed. Repentance or the acknowledgment of a mistake is not at all easy for him. Consequently, he will be more apt to make it up to those he has wronged without really facing his mistake. The worrisome traits of the phlegmatic side of his nature may so curtail his adventurous tendencies that he never quite measures up to his capabilities.

Titus, the spiritual son of the Apostle Paul and leader of the hundred or so churches on the Isle of Crete, may well have been a ChlorPhleg. When filled with the Spirit, he was the kind of man on whom Paul could depend on to faithfully teach the Word to the churches and administrate them capably for the glory of God. The book which Paul wrote to him makes ideal reading for any teacher, particularly a ChlorPhleg.

The MelSan

Mr. MelSan is usually a very gifted person, fully capable of being a musician who can steal the heart of an audience. As an artist, he not only draws or paints beautifully but can sell his own work- if he's in the right mood. It is not uncommon to encounter him in the field of education, for he makes a good scholar and probably the best of all classroom teachers, particularly on the high school and college level. The melancholy in him will ferret out little-known facts and be exacting in the use of events and detail, while the sanguine will enable him to communicate well with students.

Mr. MelSan shows an interesting combination of mood swings. Be sure of this: he is an emotional creature! When circumstances are pleasing to him, he can reflect a fantastically happy mood. But if things work out badly or he is rejected, insulted, or injured, he drops into such a mood that his lesser sanguine nature drowns in the resultant sea of self-pity. He is easily moved to tears, feels everything deeply, but can be unreasonably critical and hard on others. He tends to be rigid and usually will not cooperate unless things go his way, which is often idealistic and impractical. He is often a fearful, insecure man with a poor self-image which limits him unnecessarily.

Many of the prophets were MelSans- John the Baptist, Elijah, Jeremiah, and others. They had a tremendous capacity to commune with God, were self-sacrificing people-helpers who had enough charisma to attract a following, tended to be legalistic in their teachings and call to repentance, exhibited a flair for the dramatic, and willingly died for their principles.

The MelChlor

The mood swings of the melancholy are usually stabilized by the MelChlor's self-will and determination. There is almost nothing vocationally which this man cannot do-and do well. He is both a perfectionist and a driver. He possesses strong leadership capabilities. Almost any craft, construction, or educational level is open to him. Unlike the MelSan, he may found his own institution or business and run it capably-not with noise and color but with efficiency. Many a great orchestra leader and choral conductor is a MelChlor.

The natural weaknesses of MelChlors reveal themselves in the mind, emotions, and mouth. They are extremely difficult people to please, rarely satisfying even themselves. Once they start thinking negatively about something or someone including themselves, they can be intolerable to live with. Their mood follows their thought process. Although they do not retain a depressed mood as long as the other blends of the melancholy, they can lapse into it more quickly. The two basic temperaments haunted by self-persecution, hostility, and criticism are the melancholy and the choleric. It is not uncommon for him to get angry at God as well as his fellowman, and if such thoughts persist long enough he may become manic-depressive. In extreme cases, he can become sadistic. When confronted with his vile thinking pattern and angry, bitter spirit, he can be expected to explode.

His penchant for detailed analysis and perfection tends to make him a nitpicker who drives others up the wall. Unless he is filled with God's Spirit or can maintain a positive frame of mind, he is not enjoyable company for long periods of time. No one is more painfully aware of this than his wife and children. He not only "emotes" disapproval, but feels compelled to castigate them verbally for their failures and to correct their mistakes-in public as well as private. This man, by nature, desperately needs the love of God in his heart, and his family needs him to share it with them.

Many of the great men of the Bible show signs of a MelChlor temperament. Two that come to mind are Paul's tireless traveling companion, Dr. Luke, the painstaking scholar who carefully researched the life of Christ and left the church the most detailed account of our Lord's life, as well as the only record of the spread of the early church, and Moses, the great leader of Israel. Like many MelChlors, the latter never gained victory over his hostility and bitterness. Consequently, he died before his time. Like Moses, who wasted forty years on the backside of the desert, harboring bitterness and animosity before surrendering his life to God, many a MelChlor never lives up to his amazing potential because of the spirit of anger and revenge.

The MelPhleg

Some of the greatest scholars the world has ever known have been MelPhlegs. They are not nearly as prone to hostility as the two previous melancholies and usually get along well with others. These gifted introverts combine the analytical perfectionism of the melancholy with the organized efficiency of the phlegmatic. They are usually good-natured humanitarians who prefer a quiet, solitary environment for study and research to the endless rounds of activities sought by the more extroverted temperaments. MelPhlegs are usually excellent spellers and good mathematicians. These gifted people have greatly benefited humanity. Most of the world's significant inventions and medical discoveries have been made by MelPhlegs.

Despite his abilities, the MelPhleg, like the rest of us, has his own potential weaknesses. Unless controlled by God, he easily becomes discouraged and develops a very negative thinking pattern. But once he realizes it is a sin to develop the spirit of criticism and learns to rejoice, his entire outlook on life can be transformed. Ordinarily a quiet person, he is capable of inner angers and hostility caused by his tendency to be vengeful.

MelPhlegs are unusually vulnerable to fear, anxiety, and a negative self-image. It has always amazed me that the people with the greatest talents and capabilities are often victimized by genuine feelings of poor self-worth. Their strong tendency to be conscientious allows them to let others pressure them into making commitments that drain their energy and creativity. When filled with God's spirit, these people are loved and admired by their family because their personal self-discipline and dedication are exemplary in the home. But humanitarian concerns cause them to neglect their family. Unless they learn to pace themselves and enjoy diversions that help them relax, they often become early mortality statistics.

The most likely candidate for a MelPhleg in the Bible is the beloved Apostle John. He obviously had a very sensitive nature, for as a youth he laid his head on Jesus' breast at the Lord's Supper. On one occasion he became so angry at some people that he asked the Lord Jesus to call fire from heaven down on them. Yet at the crucifixion he was the one lone disciple who devotedly stood at the cross. John was the one to whom the dying Jesus entrusted his mother. Later the disciple became a great church leader and left us five books in the New Testament, two of which (the Gospel of John and the Book of Revelation) particularly glorify Jesus Christ.

The PhlegSan

The easiest of the twelve temperament blends to get along with over a protracted period of time is the PhlegSan. He is congenial, happy, cooperative, thoughtful, people-oriented, diplomatic, dependable, fun-loving, and humorous. A favorite with children and adults, he never displays an abrasive personality. He is usually a good family man who enjoys a quiet life and loves his wife and children. Ordinarily he attends a church where the pastor is a good motivator; there he probably takes an active role.

The weaknesses of the PhlegSan are as gentle as his personality - unless you have to live with him all the time. Since he inherited the lack of discipline of a sanguine, it is not uncommon for the PhlegSan to fall short of his true capabilities. He often quits school, passes up good opportunities, and avoids anything that involves "too much effort." Fear is another problem that accentuates his unrealistic feelings of insecurity. With more faith, he could grow beyond his timidity and self-defeating anxieties. However, he prefers to build a self-protective shell around himself and selfishly avoids the kind of involvement or commitment to activity that he needs and that would be a rich blessing to his partner and children. I have tremendous respect for the potential of these happy, contented people, but they must cooperate by letting God motivate them to unselfish activity.

The man in the Scripture that reminds me most of the PhlegSan is gentle, faithful, good-natured Timothy, the favorite spiritual son of the Apostle Paul. He was dependable and steady but timid and fearful. Repeatedly, Paul had to urge him to be more aggressive and to "do the work of an evangelist" (2 Tim. 4:5).

The PhlegChlor

The most active of all phlegmatics is the PhlegChlor. But it must be remembered that since he is predominantly a phlegmatic, he will never be a ball of fire. Like his brother phlegmatics, he is easy to get along with and may become an excellent group leader. The phlegmatic has the potential to become a good counselor, for he is an excellent listener, does not interrupt the client with stories about himself, and is genuinely interested in other people. Although the PhlegChlor rarely offers his services to others, when they come to his organized office where he exercises control, he is a first-rate professional. His advice will be practical, helpful, and - if he is a Bible-taught Christian - quite trustworthy. His gentle spirit never makes people feel threatened. He always does the right thing, rarely goes beyond the norm. If his wife can make the adjustment to his passive life-style and reluctance to take the lead in the home, particularly in the discipline of their children, they can enjoy a happy marriage.

The weaknesses of the PhlegChlor are not readily apparent but gradually come to the surface, especially in the home. In addition to the lack of motivation and the fear problems of the other phlegmatics, he can be determinedly stubborn and unyielding. He doesn't blow up at others, but simply refuses to give in or cooperate. He is not a fighter by nature, but often lets his inner anger and stubbornness reflect itself in silence. The PhlegChlor often retreats to his "workshop" alone or nightly immerses his mind in TV. The older he gets, the more he selfishly indulges his sedentary tendency and becomes increasingly passive. Although he will probably live a long and peaceful life, if he indulges these passive feelings it is a boring life - not only for him, but also for his family. He needs to give himself to the concerns and needs of his family.

No man in the Bible epitomizes the PhlegChlor better than Abraham in the Old Testament. Fear characterized everything he did in the early days. For instance, he was reluctant to leave the security of the pagan city of Ur when God first called him; he even denied his wife on two occasions and tried to palm her off as his sister because of fear. Finally, he surrendered completely to God and grew in the spirit. Accordingly, his greatest weakness became his greatest strength. Today, instead of being known as fearful Abraham, he has the reputation of being the man who "believed in the Lord; and he counted it unto him for righteousness."

The PhlegMel

Of all the temperament blends, the PhlegMel is the most gracious, gentle, and quiet. He is rarely angry or hostile and almost never says anything for which he must apologize (mainly because he rarely says much). He never embarrasses himself or others, always does the proper thing, dresses simply, and is dependable and exact. He tends to have the spiritual gifts of mercy and help, and he is neat and organized in his working habits. Like any phlegmatic, he is handy around the house and as energy permits will keep his home in good repair. If he has a wife who recognizes his tendencies toward passivity (but tactfully waits for him to take the lead in their home), they will have a good family life and marriage. However, if she resents his reticence to lead and be aggressive, she may become discontented and foment marital strife. He may neglect the discipline necessary to help prepare his children for a productive, self-disciplined life and so "provoke his children to wrath" just as much as the angry tyrant whose unreasonable discipline makes them bitter.

The other weaknesses of this man revolve around fear, selfishness, negativism, criticism, and lack of self-image. Once a PhlegMel realizes that only his fears and negative feelings about himself keep him from succeeding, he is able to come out of his shell and become an effective man, husband, and father. Most PhlegMels are so afraid of over-extending themselves or getting over involved that they automatically refuse almost any kind of affiliation.

Personally I have never seen a PhlegMel over involved in anything - except in keeping from getting over involved. He must recognize that since he is not internally motivated, he definitely needs to accept more responsibility than he thinks he can fulfill, for that external stimulation will motivate him to greater achievement. All phlegmatics work well under pressure, but it must come from outside. His greatest source of motivation, of course, will be the power of the Holy Spirit.

Barnabas, the godly saint of the first-century church who accompanied the Apostle Paul on his first missionary journey, was in all probability a PhlegMel. He was the man who gave half his goods to the early church to feed the poor, the man who contended with Paul over providing John Mark (his nephew) another chance to serve God by accompanying them on the second missionary journey. Although the contention became so sharp that Barnabas took his nephew and they proceeded on their journey by themselves, Paul later commended Mark saying, "He is profitable to me for the ministry" (2 Tim. 4:11). Today we have the Gospel of

Mark because faithful, dedicated, and gentle Barnabas was willing to help him over a hard place in his life. PhlegMels respond to the needs of others if they will just let themselves move out into the stream of life and work with people where they are.

LOOK FOR THESE OTHER TITLES FROM THE AUTHOR

Made in the USA
Columbia, SC
16 August 2022

64599306R00068